DOG TALK

by
Robert Taylor

Contents

by
Robert Taylor

Introduction

The apartment looks like a tornado had ripped through it. What, only shortly before, had been a brand new leather sofa is now a pile of springs and stuffing. The tattered remnants of a cashmere sweater lie on the floor amid the shards of a shattered glass lamp.

Strewn garbage litters the kitchen, a gnawed shoe nestles next to a shredded copy of the latest John Grisham best-seller. A flood from a punctured waterbed seeps relentlessly through the bedroom door.

In the midst of all this wreckage, sleeping peacefully, lies a dog.

At the sound of a key in the front door lock, the dog leaps to life. His tail wags, his ears prick up, his eyes laugh. The happiest moment of his day is about to unfold – his owner is coming home!

The door opens slowly into the darkened living room. A hand gropes for the light switch. The dog vibrates with gleeful anticipation.

Light bathes the room. The woman, rigid with disbelief, screams:

"Rufus! Bad dog! Bad, bad dog!"

Quick as lightning, she strides toward the dog. His ears sag, his body cringes, his eyes dodge her glinting stare and his tail curls tightly between his legs.

"Bad, bad, bad dog!" she shrieks.

Slowly, the dog's demeanor changes. His ears flatten, his tail straightens, his mouth pulls back in an angry grimace. A low growl rumbles in his throat.

Wait a minute! Isn't man (and woman, of course) and dog supposed to be the best of friends? They are, they can be, and they should be. But what we have just witnessed is a classic case of failure to communicate.

A dog and his owner find themselves on opposite sides of the language barrier and, unless they can learn to talk to each other in terms they both can understand, the rocky road they're on will only get rockier.

That's the problem. The solution is Dog Talk, the language our canine companions use to communicate with us. And this book is all you need to master it.

Dog Talk is an ancient language whose origin is lost in the mists of history. But its meanings are as clear as those of any human tongue. Once you've learned them, a whole new world will open up.

Ever wonder what's going on in your dog's mind? Sure you have. Every dog lover has. *Dog Talk* will unlock those secrets . . . and more.

You will learn to "read" your dog perfectly. You'll fully understand his moods down to the most subtle nuances. You'll be able to see the world through his eyes, feel what he feels and think the way he thinks – and, yes, dogs do think.

You'll also learn how he "reads" you so that you will never again send him mixed messages.

This mutual understanding will enrich the relationship you have with your dog and – crucially – help you to avoid the pitfalls that led to the problems between Rufus and his frustrated owner.

In the following pages, you'll gain a new appreciation of your dog's consciousness – and expand your own.

You'll come to understand how he evolved from the wild wolf. You'll grasp the intricacies of pack behavior, the social conventions that determine how your dog relates to other dogs and to you and your family.

You'll become comfortable in the role of Alpha Dog, the leader of the pack, and you'll learn how to win your dog's respect and devotion.

Dog Talk will unlock the secrets of picking the perfect puppy. It will unravel the mystery of training your dog to be happily obedient. It will provide you with the key to correcting the most common behavior problems.

Most important of all, fluency in Dog Talk will make you and your pet the best of friends and forge a loving bond between you that will last forever.

Dances With Wolves

What is a dog? It sounds like a silly question, but it's not. That little ball of fluff with the lolling tongue and laughing eyes is next of kin to an animal you'd think twice about cuddling up with – the wolf!

Your dog – yes, the one whose wagging tail greets you when you walk through the door and who dutifully fetches the newspaper from the front lawn on rainy mornings – parted company from the ravenous wolf in the great family tree of life about 12,000 to 14,000 years ago. And that, in terms of the evolution of the species, is yesterday.

Most of the genetic hard-wiring that makes the wolf such a ferociously efficient hunter is still alive and furiously firing off primordial signals in your dog's brain.

Relax. You don't have to cower in the corner. Your pup isn't harboring dark thoughts of mayhem and destruction. Twelve thousand years of domestication have modified his genetic inheritance so that he now richly deserves his title as Man's Best Friend.

But in order to understand the complex language dogs use to communicate with each other – and with

10

you – it's necessary to take stock of their heritage because it remains an important part of what they are.

Only when you make the effort to understand how millions of years have shaped the way in which your dog's senses help him cope with his environment and have enabled him to survive the harsh realities of the wild, can you fully enjoy the most rewarding relationship that exists between man and animal.

Let's spend the next few pages examining the dog's noble ancestors.

In the Beginning

It all started about 60 million years ago with a small five-toed, weasel-like animal called *Miacis*. This animal was the forebear of a family of mammals known as *Canids*, a group that today includes wolves, foxes, jackals and dogs.

An early Canid known as *Cynodictis*, a mid-size mammal with a bushy coat of fur and a long tail, first appeared approximately 35 million years ago.

As the eons passed, *Cynodictis* gave rise to *Tomarctus*, who ranged over Europe and Asia. The *Tomarctus* developed into the wolf.

Dogs as we know them evolved 14,000 years ago from a type of gray wolf that originally made his home in India, but soon spread throughout the Northern Hemisphere and eventually reached North America.

Wolves once roamed freely from the Arctic Circle to Mexico in North America and throughout Europe as far south as the Mediterranean Sea. The wolf was also common in China and the Arabian Peninsula. Sadly, he is now mostly confined to Alaska, Canada, Russia and Scandinavia.

Today, two types of wolves survive – the gray wolf (also called the timber wolf), your dog's original ancestor, and the smaller, rarer, red wolf.

The gray wolf is a large, powerful, predatory animal. He can grow up to 6 feet in length (including his tail) and weigh as much as 175 pounds.

Long, dense fur protects him from sub-zero temperatures. His massive jaws and savage fangs make him an extremely efficient hunter.

His diet consists of large animals like deer and moose, which he stalks relentlessly over hundreds of miles, mostly at night. But he can survive on mice and other small rodents when his preferred prey proves too elusive.

By now, you're probably asking: What does this savage lord of the wilderness have to do with the cute little puppy frolicking in my lap and affectionately licking my face?

The answer is this: They're both intensely intelligent and highly social animals. These two traits form the basis of how successfully you and your dog will be able to communicate with each other.

Running with the Pack

Wolves live in packs. Even though tales of the solitary "lone wolf" have worked their way into popular mythology and fiction, a wolf cut off from his pack – his society – is a wretched creature whose only goal is to rejoin his pals or attach himself to another pack.

A pack is usually an extended family group of up to two dozen individuals, composed of a male and female, their offspring of various ages and hangers-on.

Pack behavior is governed by clearly defined social rules that all members understand.

Each pack has a dominant male and female (the Alpha Pair) and only they have the right to mate. Young wolves stay with the pack until they are about 2 years old, then they set off to search for mates of their own, becoming the leaders of a new pack.

The Alpha Male calls the shots and fiercely fights off challengers to his authority. But the pack usually lives in harmony because all its members understand the social laws that govern it. And they learn what these laws are from their elders because wolves are masters of communication – totally fluent in the language of the pack.

Animal trainer Bash Dibra, who once molded a wolf cub into a movie star, has identified the key rules of pack behavior. In his book, *Dog Speak* (Simon & Schuster), he says: "The driving force that governs all wolf behavior, the Code of the Pack, has found its way down the genetic line to encode the behavior of dogs as well."

In other words, your playful little pet sees the world though a wolf's eyes.

To understand your dog, you must first understand how he carries in his genes the same language of the pack that governs the way wolves behave.

Learning the laws of the pack is the first step in learning to speak the language that your dog uses to communicate with you and the language you must learn to successfully join in the conversation.

The Leader of the Pack

A wolf pack is not a democracy. Its members don't get to vote on whether to chase a moose or a caribou on any given day. . . or whether to hunt at all.

Individual wolves don't eat when they are hungry or sleep when they are tired. If there are young to be cared for, they all must do their share.

The pack has no patience with those who don't follow the rules. Its survival depends on a tightly regulated social system and free-spirits are quickly, and sometimes brutally, brought into line.

Only one wolf calls the shots and he is an absolute monarch, a tyrant who fought for the power he wields and will fight to protect his position at the head of the pack until he is too old and feeble to fight anymore.

Once the Alpha Wolf has established his dominance, the other wolves willingly follow his lead. Bred into their genes is the knowledge that without him, the pack as a group would not survive, nor would they survive alone.

The Alpha's leadership guarantees successful hunting, safety from predators and a secure environment for raising the next generations that will ensure the survival of the pack.

The Alpha Male rules with the Alpha Female, who

14

keeps other female members of the pack in line. She is responsible for choosing the all-important location of the den – the center of pack life and the hub around which all activities revolve.

The other members of the pack, called Beta Wolves, assume submissive positions in this rigidly hierarchical society.

The Wolf Within

By now, it probably seems as though you've picked up a copy of the course notes for Wolf Behavior 101. But there's an important point in all of this:

Although thousands of years of domestication have taken your dog out of the pack, the pack mentality is still very alive in your dog. It's still there in the DNA that makes your dog a dog.

When you bring a dog into your home, you and your family become his pack. He immediately looks for an Alpha presence – and you are it – or should be. If he senses a leadership vacuum in the family-pack, he will try to fill it. If he succeeds, you will have to fight to establish control.

In other words, if you and your dog are to have a rewarding life together, you must establish yourself as the Alpha presence from the beginning.

If you do, your dog will readily accept his Beta status and show you more love, respect and loyalty than you dreamed possible in a relationship.

Unlike the Alpha Wolf, you won't have to fend off periodic attacks on your authority, but you must be firm in establishing and maintaining your authority if you want to prevent your dog from becoming a juvenile delinquent who will be a pain in your neck rather than a joy in your heart.

Fortunately, your dog has inherited from his wolf ancestors an agile brain that has been programmed – in a sense – to make communication easy.

His hard-wiring includes the ability to send, receive and decode a wide variety of messages. By the time you've read this book, you'll know just the right moves to make to assert yourself as the leader of your pack without upsetting your dog or sending mixed signals he won't be able to understand.

As with so much else about the modern domestic canine, Dog Talk has its origins in the way wolves exchange information necessary to the survival of the pack.

Wolf-Talk

The intricate society of the wolf pack is held together by an extraordinarily complex system of communication. The Alpha Wolf doesn't beat around the bush. He lets the others know what he wants through

Why does a dog's hair stand on end?

A dog's hair bristles when he's frightened or feels he's being aggressively challenged. It's a way of making himself look bigger and more intimidating to the other dog – or human – he feels is threatening him. It's how canines puff out their chests to look more macho.

a precise series of instructions conveyed in Wolf-Talk, a combination of vocal cues and body language.

The other wolves don't need a dictionary to sort out what the Alpha Wolf means. Their brains are genetically structured to interpret his barks, facial expressions and other physical gestures just as he is programmed to transmit them.

This language of the wolves is the same language your dog speaks and, if the two of you are ever going to communicate successfully, you will have to learn it.

Don't worry. As you'll soon discover, it's a lot easier to master than French.

Life with Lobo

Before leaving the wonderful world of wolves, there are a few more facts of pack life that you should understand because they play a role in determining how your dog reacts to his world – and interacts with you.

Wolves are aggressive. If they didn't hunt and kill, they'd die. Your dog has inherited that aggression, and if you don't channel it into acceptable avenues, you'll have a canine criminal on your hands.

They hunt by chasing and running down their prey, so if you don't want your dog to treat the neighbor's cat as a dinner-time delicacy, you'll have to take charge.

Food is scarce in the wilderness, obtained only by risking life and limb. So wolves protect their portion of the kill ferociously. In a similar way, your dog will be fiercely protective of his food bowl – and eternally grateful to you as his only food source.

In the wild, wolves jealously guard their territory. Fido will exhibit that same territoriality when it comes to your neighborhood, your house and even those parts of your house that he regards as his special turf.

Although wolves are fearless fighters, they aren't fools. When they perceive that the odds are stacked against them, they flee. This flight instinct, if you don't control it, can lead your dog to run into traffic . . . and tragedy.

As we already know, nature has seen to it that the Alpha Wolf is a master communicator. By learning the tricks of his trade, you will become the Alpha presence your dog needs to reach his full potential as a pet, a protector and a pal.

Man's Best Friend

No one knows for sure when humans and dogs entered into one of history's most inspiring examples of co-op-eration between man and nature, but the fossil record indicates that it happened about 14,000 years ago.

We were living in caves, scrounging for food by throwing rocks and pointed sticks at small animals. Wolves and wild dogs would skulk around our campfires, literally waiting for us to toss them a bone. Fossil remains showed that sometimes they preyed on young and feeble humans and also that we hunted them as food in times of need.

It soon occurred to our

caveman ancestors that man and wolf would both benefit by helping each other out.

We could use their speed, awesome sense of smell and "team mentality" to locate prey too clever or swift for man to catch on our own. We could then take advantage of our simple weapons to minimize the risk involved in finishing off the kill. And we could all share in the bounty.

We also discovered that canines possess acute hearing. That, combined with their instinctual urge to protect the security of the pack at all costs, qualified them for guard duty around our primitive camps.

Our enemies, whether predatory animals or rival tribes of cavemen, became their enemies.

Thus developed a working relationship between man and canine. As we became more civilized and moved from hunting and gathering to farming and raising animals for food and clothing, that relationship deepened.

We learned that our canine colleagues, with a little instruction, could herd our flocks. We learned that the biggest and strongest would willingly serve as beasts of burden, carrying crops from the field to our granaries.

For their part, they extended their notion of the pack to embrace their new human allies. We began to see that they were intelligent, loyal and ready to please.

We also figured out that by mating canines with similar physical traits and aptitudes to each other, we could make them even more useful by enhancing the qualities that best suited certain tasks. In so doing, we created the more than 125 breeds of dog that make up the canine family we have come to love and value so much.

Of course, through selective breeding, we bred away some of their natural instincts.

You'd have a hard time, for example, training a Doberman pinscher, bred to guard and protect, to herd your cattle. Similarly, a sheep dog put on guard duty would be more likely to herd a band of thieves than scare them off.

As we shall see, this creates a special set of training problems for certain breeds. But it remains true that all modern dogs share the basic pack characteristics of the wolves that preceded them on the evolutionary totem pole.

And one of those traits is the ability to send and receive an astonishingly large number of messages. It is this "language" that makes them so trainable and, if we learn it, opens up a whole new level of intimacy between our dogs and ourselves.

How Smart Is Your Dog?

If you ever ask a dog owner how smart his or her pet is, be prepared to hear a long list of accomplishments that would turn Einstein green with IQ envy. Rare is the canine lover who doesn't think her little Poopsie is a card-carrying member of Mensa, the organization of eggheads who make the rest of us feel less than smart by scoring off the scale on intelligence quizzes.

But evaluating "dog smarts" is a tricky business. We tend to dismiss them either as mindlessly responding to external stimuli, much like a computer does, or we try to judge their intelligence by comparison with our own. Both approaches are wrong.

Any person who has paid close attention while observing a dog figure out where his owner has hidden a treat knows that there is a lot more going on between his ears than the meshing of preprogrammed gears.

On the other hand, whatever feats of brilliance a dog may be capable of, he can't make his mental states known to us by manipulating the words and visual images that form the basis of human intelligence tests.

Your intuition that your dog is bright is not unfounded. If you ever run into a skeptic, or if you're a closet skeptic yourself, try this little exercise.

Read down the following list of familiar names:

Jerry Seinfeld
Lisa Kudrow
Robert DeNiro
Susan Sarandon
Mary Martin
Dustin Hoffman
Julia Roberts
Martin Sheen
Robert Redford

Now, close the book and recite them in the order in which they're printed. Repeat the process until you – or your skeptical friend – get it right.

How many tries did it take? If it took 10 or more, don't go looking for a dunce cap. Most people, even very clever ones, need at least that many times to recall the list.

Now, how many times must a reasonably bright dog be walked through one of the five basic obedience school exercises – sit, stay, heel, come, down – before getting it down pat? About five! Some of them get it the very first time if the trainer is fluent in Dog Talk.

That should be enough to send the skeptics running for cover – and to let you know that when you're deal-

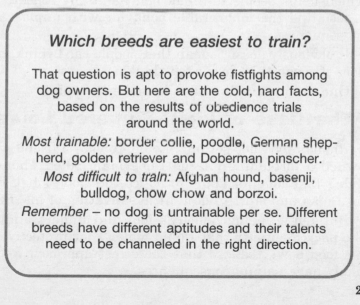

ing with your dog, you're dealing with a pretty smart critter.

Canine intelligence has gotten a bum rap ever since the 17th century French philosopher Rene Descartes decided, for whatever reason, that dogs didn't have souls, which he believed contained the intellect as well as the spirit.

For Descartes, a dog was nothing more than a sophisticated and somewhat mysterious machine.

Descartes was led to this conclusion by a complicated series of rational deductions, but there is good evidence suggesting that deep down in his dog-lovin' heart he didn't believe his own theory. He had a pampered pet pooch and he used to chat cheerfully with it all day long.

Which breeds are easiest to train?

That question is apt to provoke fistfights among dog owners. But here are the cold, hard facts, based on the results of obedience trials around the world.

Most trainable: border collie, poodle, German shepherd, golden retriever and Doberman pinscher.

Most difficult to train: Afghan hound, basenji, bulldog, chow chow and borzoi.

Remember – no dog is untrainable per se. Different breeds have different aptitudes and their talents need to be channeled in the right direction.

However, others did believe it and the theory is alive and well today in a school of psychological thought called behaviorism, which says that dogs – along with other animals – don't think at all, but merely react instinctively to promptings from their environment.

The most famous example is the Russian experimenter Pavlov, who taught laboratory dogs to associate feeding time with the ringing of a bell.

Once the pattern had been firmly established, Pavlov found that the dogs would salivate every time they heard a bell ring, even if there was no reward to follow.

That's all well and good. The same techniques of positive and negative reinforcement work on humans, too. They're the theoretical foundation of *aversion therapy* which helps people to break bad habits by repeatedly associating the undesirable behavior with unpleasant consequences.

It obviously doesn't mean that people can't think, nor does it mean that dogs can't think.

One example, will suffice to make the point.

The Case of Light-Fingered Louie

Rhonda took her pet pug, Louie, to visit a friend who owned a forbiddingly large Doberman called Thor. It didn't take long for Louie to notice the Dobie's half-full food dish and start to do a little salivating of his own.

But Louie, being nobody's fool and understanding the pack mentality that would make Thor protective of his food bowl, realized that the direct approach would likely have painful consequences.

So he waited until Thor's back was turned, staged a lightning raid and escaped to the living room with a single kernel of food in his mouth. Temporarily safe, he paused to munch the morsel.

Puffed up by his success, Louie darted at the bowl and snatched a second kernel of Thor's food. This time, however, not wanting to push his luck, he ran into a bedroom with his loot.

Louie repeated this pattern – one kernel to the living room, the next to the bedroom – over and over until Thor's bowl was empty.

He had never visited this house before, had never laid eyes on Thor or Thor's food bowl. What Louie had done was size up the situation, recognize that Thor represented a threatening obstacle to his desire to clean out the food bowl, and figure out a way to accomplish his goal while avoiding detection.

In other words, Louie worked out a plan – and that requires a great deal of what psychologists call *adaptive intelligence*, one of the highest and most thought-out forms of human mental activity.

Louie, like Descartes, was a thinker.

But before we rush out to grant Rover a Ph.D., let's be clear about what a dog can – and cannot – do.

If only my dog could talk...

Dog Talk

Two aspects of human intelligence are closed books as far as dogs are concerned. As agile as their minds are, dogs can't play with words or numbers.

Even the smartest dog in the world can't make a speech or solve a differential equation. He'll never add two and two or say, feed me. (But remember, Einstein had difficulty balancing his checkbook.)

That said, modern researchers have accepted that dogs do share three crucial forms of intelligence with humans:

1. They can learn from their experiences and apply the knowledge they've accumulated to new situations in order to solve new problems. They can also grasp instructions and know what they have to do in order to carry them out.

2. And even though they don't use words, they can communicate. In fact, using the tools at their disposal – sounds and body language – they can convey an astonishing amount of information. They've inherited this ability from their wolf cousins, who need to communicate extensively with each other to maintain the social cohesion of the pack.

26

3. Furthermore, even though dogs can't utter words, they can certainly understand them. Researchers estimate that the average pet has a comprehension vocabulary of about 60 human words and simple phrases. Some prodigies can grasp the meaning of more than 300 everyday words!

In his book, *The Intelligence of Dogs* (Bantam), psychologist and dog trainer Stanley Coren identifies another type of intelligence that dogs possess, without which they would never have become our favorite animal companions.

Dogs exhibit a high degree of interactive, or social intelligence. Their ability to scope out situations and figure out the role they're expected to play is uncanny, a holdover from the wolf pack where observation of hierarchical status was necessary to survival.

Dogs have the ability to pay attention to each other and to the members of their human pack. They are always alertly probing their surroundings for clues and signals.

They're especially attuned to those signs that appear as cues to specific types of behavior. In a pack, they look to the Alpha to dictate the action; in the home, they look to you – if you've established yourself as the Alpha Presence.

Amazingly, they're also capable of forgiveness. A resentful wolf makes a lousy pack member and a resentful dog makes a lousy companion.

But if you are as consistent in the signals you give as the Alpha, your dog will readily overlook minor slip-ups. The key is to reestablish a consistent and predictable pattern of behavior as soon as possible.

The other side of this coin is that your dog will be scrupulously consistent in the signals he sends to you. If you pay attention to him, the two of you will quickly achieve a level of communication in which misunderstandings will be few and relatively minor.

The range of signals that your dog will learn to respond to is very wide and, to a large extent, the two of you can work out your own "language."

But a word of caution – a very important one – is in order. Your dog's genetic hard-wiring predisposes him to respond to certain gestures in certain quite specific ways. No matter how much time you spend with him, no matter how many training sessions you have together, you'll never be able to change this.

You must work within the parameters that nature has imposed on your pet. He will interpret a quickly raised hand as a threatening gesture no matter how hard you try to make it mean something else.

If you were traveling in France and wanted directions to the bus station, you'd get a better result if you asked the question in French rather than English.

The same holds true when you try to talk to your dog – you must make an attempt to speak his "language."

You don't have to be perfect. Your pet's adaptive intelligence will enable him to smooth out the rough spots. But you must give him half a chance to understand what you're trying to communicate to him and you'll never do that if you fail to observe the basics rules of Dog Talk.

What Is Your Dog Saying to You?

Your dog has a rich vocabulary that he uses to talk to you. With it, he can express a wide range of emotions and desires. The message can be simple, like: "Feed me!" Or, it can be complex: "I've missed you and I'd really like you to play with me – now!"

You probably understand much of your dog's language already. Only the most dense of dog owners would need to be told twice that grabbing the leash and pawing at the doorknob means: "I want to go out."

But not all canine signals are so simple, and serious misunderstandings can occur. That's where a few Dog Talk basics become helpful.

For example, Jane returns home from a long day at the office to find that her poodle, Primrose, has pushed her way into the closet and transformed a favorite cashmere sweater into a tattered rag fit only for dusting the furniture.

A stranger to Dog Talk, Jane interprets Primrose's act as a willful act of canine vandalism and taps her across the snout with a rolled-up copy of a magazine.

Primrose didn't spend her day scouring the house for opportunities to get into mischief. What she was saying to Jane is this: "You left me alone and I missed you terribly. Since I couldn't be near you, I found the something that reminded me of you. Your sweater had your scent, the scent I love, all over it. Since I couldn't play with you, I played with the next best thing I could find."

Scents and Sensitivity

Your dog's nose is 100 times more sensitive than yours. He can detect substances 100 million times more dilute than you can.

The part of your dog's brain that enables him to process scent data is 14 times larger than man's – in fact, it's the most highly developed part of the canine neurological system.

Your dog's sense of smell is so good, it's one of the great wonders of nature. Like so many other things about him, it's a trait he's inherited from his wolf ancestors – one that was essential to their survival.

A wolf's nose is so sensitive he can use it to distinguish each and every member of his pack. He can identify animals by their scent when they are a mile and a half away.

That's why your dog keeps his nose close to the ground when you take him for an outing. Its his way of discovering what's been going on in the neighborhood since his last walk.

One whiff of days-old urine in the grass can tell him the age and sex of the dog who left it. It's subtle nuances also reveal the stranger's frame of mind – aggressive dogs leave different scents from submissive ones – and even the state of his health.

When it comes to humans, his nose can tell him if you're angry or happy, paying attention to him or distracted. And, yes, they can smell fear.

Because she didn't understand Dog Talk, Jane misinterpreted an act of devotion for an act of hostility. When she punished Primrose by swatting her with the latest issue of *Newsweek*, she compounded the miscommunication by giving the dog strong negative feedback for what, to the canine mind, seemed like a positive gesture.

Primed in Dog Talk, Jane would have understood Primrose's behavior as a cry of loneliness and taken the appropriate steps to make the dog's life a little more comfortable during her absences.

She might, for example, choose to leave an old, unwanted piece of clothing near Primrose's bed so the pooch would have something to remember her by without having to break into the closet. On another level, she might also learn to close the closet door firmly before leaving the house!

Sometimes failing to understand Dog Talk can have tragic consequences. When Mike brought home Rufus the rottweiler as a puppy, his wife Lois enjoyed roughhousing with the new addition to their family.

As Rufus grew – and grew and grew – his playing became more and more aggressive. Lois wouldn't admit it, but she was actually a little intimidated by her increasingly powerful playmate.

The first time Rufus got too rambunctious, she calmed him down by giving him a doggy treat. As the days went by, he became more and more aggressive. Soon, a handful of treats wouldn't pacify him.

Eventually, he began to menace Lois every time she

walked through the door. When Mike was there, Rufus was on his best behavior, but when Lois was alone with him, he turned into the Rottie from hell.

Soon, life with Rufus became unbearable for Lois and she put her foot down – with Mike, not the dog. The result: Rufus ended up with a one-way ticket to the pound.

Lois failed to understand one of the most deeply ingrained forms of canine communication. When puppies play, they're not just having fun. They're also sending out, and receiving, an incredibly complex set of signals designed to settle the crucial canine issue of dominance and submission.

While Lois was playing with Rufus, he was testing her. When she began to act submissively in the face of his challenges to her authority, it reinforced his macho self-image as the Alpha Dog in the pack.

Worse, she actually rewarded his displays of dominance by giving the conquering hero dog biscuits. By this point, it was too late: No Alpha Dog will willingly relinquish his position at the top of the totem pole.

Dog's have three basic ways of speaking to us: their body language, their facial expressions and their voices. Just as humans take basic, simple sentences and weave them into more complex statements, dogs use their basic forms of communication in combination with each other to convey more intricate messages.

In other words, a wagging tail combined with forward pointing ears and a raised head means something different from each of those gestures taken individually.

Once you grasp the basics, you shouldn't have any trouble understanding these canine "compound sentences."

The Basic Language of Dogs

TAIL

Tails are the first things people notice about dogs. Maybe it's because we don't have them ourselves or maybe it's because of their amazing expressiveness.

A wagging tail has become a symbol of happiness, contentment and friendship. But when a dog wags his tail, it can mean much, much more.

Dogs use their tails to let the world know what's on their minds in three distinct ways: motion, position and shape. With other dogs, it's one of the primary ways of establishing who stands where in the pecking order. With us, it speaks eloquently about moods, emotions and intentions.

Dogs with longer tails are at an advantage – the signals they send are easier to see and, consequently, more difficult to misinterpret. But even dogs with closely docked tails still use them to talk to us. You just have to pay closer attention.

First, let's look at the tail in motion:

Minimal, tentative wag

This is primarily a greeting. It implies that the dog is relaxed, but alert. There's no threat implied, rather a sense of anticipation. It's your move and the dog is waiting to see what you'll do.

The dog is comfortable and happy, but he's looking for some action.

He's letting you know that he expects something pleasant to happen – a walk, dinner, a play session or just an enthusiastic pat on the head. Respond in some way or your pet will be disappointed.

This is the type of tail action typically seen among young wolves and puppies when they are playing with their litter mates in a carefree way.

Slow wag, with the tail slightly lowered

The dog is asking a question. You've done or said something he doesn't quite understand. He wants to respond, but doesn't know what you expect of him. Restate your message, more emphatically or in a slightly different way.

In the wild, wolves often use this tail gesture while sizing up another wolf. You will also see a version of it when two dogs meet. It's not a prelude to a confrontation, just a wait-and-see tactic that tells the other dog to relax and explore the situation a little further.

Slight tremor, with tail held vertically erect

This is the sign of a dominant dog and a warning that a challenge to his authority might provoke an aggressive response. The dog is issuing a quiet challenge to your authority, so a decisive, but calm, expression of your superiority is required.

If the dog knows the basic obedience commands, a firm "Sit" would be an appropriate response.

Rapid wagging through a narrow range of motion with the tail held very low

The dog is conveying a signal of submission. He's acknowledging that you are in charge and that he is prepared to listen to you.

Among wolves, this gesture often avoids a nasty confrontation with an aggressive Alpha.

Now, let's turn to the equally important position of the tail:

Slightly below vertical, still

The dog is projecting a high degree of alertness. Something, maybe you, has got his attention. A wolf or hunting dog will often put his tail in this position when he hears something, but has not yet identified the sound.

Parallel to the ground and rigid

This is a sign that a challenge has been acknowledged and accepted. Your dog may be about to test your Alpha position. If he's dealing with another dog, he senses Alpha vibes and is letting the potential rival know that he's not going to knuckle under easily.

Vertical or almost vertical

No doubt about this message. The dog is letting everyone know that he is the leader of the pack – or thinks he is. This is not a threat, but the gesture of a very confident canine.

The signal should be taken seriously, though, both by humans and other dogs. If this dog is going to be told he's not the boss, it's going to have to be done diplomatically or a fight may very well ensue.

In some breeds, the husky, for example, the tail may curve over the dog's back when he wants to project this dominant posture.

Loose and a bit lower than parallel to the ground

This is a sign of a relaxed and happy dog, who's content with the way things are going. It's the normal tail position among wolves, both dominant and submissive, when they have accepted their respective places in the social hierarchy.

Low, swaying slightly

Your dog is trying to tell you that he's feeling under the weather. It could indicate something physical, but more likely it reflects that the dog is uncertain or just plain down in the dumps (it happens – dogs do get the blahs now and then, just like the rest of us).

A little reassurance is in order. If you have the time, take him for a short walk or play with him for a few minutes.

Tucked between the legs

A tell-tale (so-to-speak) sign of flat-out fear. This is way more than submission. He's probably expecting to be beaten, either by a human or a rival dog. In a wolf pack, he would be the Omega Wolf (omega is the last letter of the Greek alphabet), and no self-respecting wolf wants to be an Omega.

If you've caused your dog to behave like this, you're doing something wrong. Examine the signals you're sending to make sure you're not telegraphing a dire threat. Something in the dog's memory is telling him that a catastrophe is about to befall him.

If you rescued your pet from the pound, it's a clear indication that his previous owners abused him and he needs special handling.

But don't give in to the temptation to "baby" him. That will only reinforce the submissive behavior that you're trying to correct. What he's looking for is the structure and security that a good training program, such as you'll find here, can provide.

While he looks pathetic, and every fiber of your being is urging you to rush over to comfort the poor creature, be careful. A seriously frightened dog is often dangerous and may lash out with his teeth to protect himself if he perceives sudden movement in his direction.

Take it easy and approach him slowly. Extend your hand very tentatively with the palm open and the fingers relaxed. Speak to him in soft, reassuring tones.

If he continues to behave in this way, and doesn't respond to your best efforts to make him feel more comfortable through a reasonable training program, consider seeking the help of a professional dog handler.

Both your dog's happiness and your own depend on getting this situation under control.

STANCE

How a dog stands speaks volumes about how he

feels. When he's confident, he stands tall and proud, displaying his body at its full height. When he's nervous or fearful, he crouches ever so slightly, almost as though he's trying to make himself less conspicuous.

An extremely frightened or insecure dog will crouch and cower, trying to make himself seem as nonthreatening to others as he can.

Within this general range of stances, there are certain specific poses and postures that carry special meanings.

Leaning forward on rigid legs

He's responding to a perceived challenge or threat and letting his potential adversary know there's no way he's going to back down.

If, when meeting, two dogs both adopt this stance, the fur may be about to fly. If your dog tries this with you, he's testing you to discover how serious you are about being the Alpha Factor in the canine-human equation.

Rolling over

This is a submissive gesture, common among Beta Wolves when they're in the presence of the Alpha. It doesn't express fear, just a healthy respect for authority.

When your dog rolls over and shows you his tummy in a loose and casual way, he's telling you that he accepts your dominance – and that's a good thing.

But if the gesture is accompanied by whimpering or trembling, it's gone beyond normal dominant-submissive behavior. In extreme cases, a very cowed or terrified dog will even urinate involuntarily.

One paw raised

This can happen when the dog is either standing or sitting and it usually means that the dog is feeling uncertain about something. Something in the situation is making the dog unsure of himself or of what will happen next.

Usually, once the situation has resolved itself and the dog has a more clear understanding of what's going to unfold or what's expected of him, the paw will slowly return to the floor and it will be business as usual again.

Head or paw on the back or neck of another dog

This gesture is a classic sign of dominance, frequently seen among wolves. The two rivals have resolved the issues between them and the dominant one is confirming his status by placing his paw on the submissive dog.

Head or paw on a human knee

It would seem logical that this also would be a dominant posture, but it's not. Rather, it's just an attention-getting device. If you ignore it, be prepared for more energetic pawing, but don't interpret it as a challenge to your authority.

EYES

As with humans, the eyes are the windows to a dog's soul. They're an expressive and important component of canine communication.

Wide open, alert

The dog is conveying an attitude of happiness and friendliness. He's eager for you to pay attention to him. He's in a good mood, but he's also up to a challenge and expects you to respond firmly.

This is also the look dogs get just before they take off in hot pursuit of the latest object of their curiosity, so be careful if this happens out-of-doors – Fido might be about to dart after the neighbor's cat or into traffic.

Staring

This is the Alpha Gaze of a dog who thinks he's in charge. He means business. This is no time to let your guard down. You're being challenged and if you don't take the reins, expect to have to deal with some kind of misbehavior.

When two dogs stare intently at each other, you're headed for a showdown. Do what you can to keep them far enough apart to prevent a fight.

Blinking

Your dog has turned into a sly coquette who's flirting with you. He's letting you know that he's ready to play and frolic.

If you're in the mood to join in, fine. But even if he catches you with this canine "wink" just as you're on the way out the door, try to give him a few minutes of attention so he won't take out his frustration on the furniture after you've gone.

Dogs are like people is this regard – they don't like it when their come-hither signals are ignored. If you don't have time to romp, at least put him through a few basic obedience exercises just to let him know you care.

Looking anywhere but at you

The eyes are sending a submissive message. You'll often see this look if the dog has picked up the vibration that you're going to punish him for something.

If you notice this timid, cowering eye signal often, examine how you and your dog have been interacting to make sure your voice and gestures haven't become too intimidating. Dogs want to co-operate, but they don't like being bullied and will come to act resentfully – even snappishly – if they feel they're being pushed around. In dog-to-dog encounters, the dog that behaves this way is trying to avoid a fight he doesn't believe he can win.

Narrow, menacing

These eyes are expressing raw, naked aggression. Hopefully, you'll never see this look in your dog, but if you meet a canine stranger with this threatening glint in his eyes, be cautious.

Don't make any sudden moves that he could interpret as the onset of aggression. A dog with narrowed eyes is not about to back down. And don't turn tail and run. You'll just trigger his chase instincts and he's a heck of a lot faster on his feet than you.

Be calm, look him steadily in the face, keep your hands by your sides and slowly – very slowly – start to back away. If the dog makes a move toward you, stop until he does then repeat the process. When you convince him that you aren't a threat, he'll begin to relax.

EARS

Ears, like tails, can be a little hard to read. Severely cropped ears and long, floppy ones exhibit the same characteristics as those that are naturally erect. You just have to look a little harder to grasp subtle differences.

Standing straight up or inclined a little forward

The dog is expressing curiosity. Usually, this is in response to a sound he has yet to identify, but the same ear position indicates attention to any new event in his environment, whether the message reaches him through his ears, his eyes or his nose.

He often displays the degree of his interest and curiosity by tilting his head to one side – the greater the tilt, the greater the intensity or difficulty he is experiencing.

If he's responding to something you've said or done, he's asking you to be clearer. Make sure the tone of your voice and your gestures express the same mood. After all, you would be confused if someone barked the words "I love you" in your direction in the voice of a drill sergeant!

This ear position is the one wolves use to let each other know that the hunt is about to begin. So be wary. Your dog might be about to bolt.

Pulled back flat against the head

This is an expression of fear common to many animals, stemming from an instinct to protect their body parts from attack. In this case, the dog is reflexively

42

trying to get his ears out of the way of whatever he perceives to be threatening him.

In any event, something is scaring the dog and he's buying time while considering his course of action. Will he fight? Will he flee? Or will he submissively roll over on his back?

Talk to him in a soothing, reassuring voice until the wave of fear begins to go away. Then, put him through a quick obedience drill to let him know it's business as usual.

Never comfort him by offering him a treat. It will only reinforce his tendency to react timidly in uncertain surroundings. You don't want an overly aggressive dog, but neither do you want to nurture a wimp.

And don't make any sudden moves – aggression is one method dogs resort to when faced with something frightening.

Back a little, but not tight against the head

This is a mild signal of discontent and the mood will usually pass by itself without any intervention on your part. If the dog's ill-at-ease feeling intensifies, his ears will let you know by becoming flush to his head, as described above.

MOUTH

In dogs, the mouth and the muzzle move in tandem. To fully understand what your pooch is trying to convey by the position of his lips, you must also pay attention to what he's doing with the flexible and expressive muscles that run along the sides of his nose.

Lips curled, teeth bared, muzzle wrinkled

This is a no-brainer. The dog is mad as heck and he's not going to take it any more.

Among wolves, this is a signal the Alpha sends to let a challenger know that he's been pushed to the limit and is about to fight to reaffirm his dominant position in the pack.

When a dog puts on this snarling face, he's making an equally bold statement. He's drawn his line in the sand – step over it and you'll feel his wrath where it's apt to leave a lasting impression.

Now is not the time to assert your Alpha authority. Be calm and firm rather than threatening and you'll disarm the situation.

When the dog relaxes, subtly reassume your position in the driver's seat by running him through a few obedience tasks until he willingly accepts you as Numero Uno.

If you encounter two dogs staring each other down with this tell-tale look on their faces, don't get between them or you'll end up the loser.

Dogs know how to settle things among themselves and very few dog fights ever result in serious injury. The loser usually assumes a submissive posture early enough in the confrontation to avoid bloodshed.

Yawn

Nope, appearances to the contrary, your dog isn't bored. He's miffed. This is a typical error that results from trying to read your dog as if he were a human being.

Yawning seems to be a canine reflex reaction to stress. Among wolves in a stand-off situation, it's not uncommon to see one of them yawn gapingly.

This is hardly a human response to a threat. Yet, it happens all the time in the wolf world and the wolf on the receiving end certainly doesn't interpret it as a sign of boredom in his rival. Rather, it puts him even more on guard and, should your dog yawn at you, you should break the tension by relaxing your own body posture, slowing down your gestures and speaking in a low, soft voice.

Mouth pulled back, with no bared teeth or wrinkled muzzle

A submissive dog will do this to let the challenging canine know that a fight is not in the cards. If the aggressor continues to menace, look for a more obvious display of submission like rolling over.

This subtle signal is often difficult for humans to read, but it's usually accompanied by other clues to the dog's state of mind.

Mouth open, teeth somewhat bared, but no snarling

The dog is letting you know that he's protecting his turf. You're apt to see it if you get too close to his food dish while he's eating.

It, too, is a throwback to wolf behavior. Dominant animals get to eat first and jealously protect their right to do so. Some dogs can get downright ornery at dinnertime and may snap at a perceived threat to their food supply. If there are kids around, it's important to teach them to respect the area around the food bowl as the dog's private space.

Mouth pulled back, lips tightly closed

Dogs experiencing mild anxiety often behave this way. If his nervousness increases, he may start to pant or salivate.

It's a low-key sign to tone down the intensity of whatever is happening between you and your pet. Give him a little room to breathe and he'll be back to himself in no time.

Smile

Yes, you were right all along, dogs do smile! And they do it in the same circumstances that we do – when they're relaxed and happy. You know the look. The mouth is relaxed and loose and the tongue may protrude a little.

It happens most often in the carefree days of puppyhood, and you'll rarely see this expression on the face of an adult wolf. But adult domestic dogs retain their playfulness all their lives.

When your dog flashes you this unmistakable look, it can be a prelude to one of those special moments when the two of you seem to be bonded by a psychic link. Take advantage of it by indulging in a little gentle playing. It will bring the two of you closer together.

VOICE

The dog's amazing ability to communicate is not con-

fined to body language. Like us, they also use their voices to transmit information.

In fact, the canine voice is an extremely wide-ranging and flexible instrument. When used together with facial expressions, stance and tail and ear position, it gives the dog an extensive and richly expressive vocabulary.

What they lack in words, they amply make up for with barks, growls, howls, whines and whimpers.

When interpreting these vocal signals, it's vital to pay attention to the pitch of the sounds your dog emits.

An unfriendly or unhappy dog will "speak" in a low register. A contented, playful one will utter a higher-pitched range of sounds.

Repetition also plays a role – the more frequently and rapidly a sound is repeated, the more urgent is the message the dog is trying to convey.

Also remember that individual breeds – even individual dogs – sound different from one another.

You have to pay attention to the sounds of your own pet before you can build up the necessary Dog Talk "recognition vocabulary" to keep the two of you happily on the same wavelength.

BARKS

Loud and frequent

This is the crow of a dominant dog, announcing to the world that he's ruler of the roost. He's like a political leader proclaiming his power from a podium.

This bark need not be directed at any particular

47

challenge to the Alpha's authority. It's a general statement to all within earshot.

Loud and frequent, accompanied by a snarl

Now's the time to watch your step. The top dog thinks he's being challenged and is announcing a readiness to fight the interloper.

Rapid, crisp, continuous

This is how wolves warn the pack there's a potential danger in the neighborhood. Your dog will bark in this fashion to let you know a stranger is approaching.

He's not threatening you – or anyone else – just doing his duty as guardian of your home and hearth, one of the first duties domesticated dogs performed for their primitive masters.

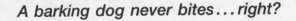

A barking dog never bites...right?

Wrong.
This is a myth that can lead to bloodshed. A short, single crisply delivered bark is a no-nonsense Dog Talk statement indicating that Rover is annoyed and may be ready to use his teeth to let you know just how upset he is.

The bark will become lower and lower in pitch as the stranger nears. If you detect a frantic edge creeping in to your dog's voice, he's probably wondering why you aren't responding to his warning.

Rapid, crisp, one or two barks only

This is a greeting bark, reserved only for those who the dog is familiar with and at ease with. It's probably the way he welcomes you home from work or announces the arrival of a family member or frequent visitor.

High-pitched, playful, repeated three or four times

The dog is happy and wants to share his good mood with you. A friendly tousle will earn you a lick of gratitude and a wag of the tail.

Very high-pitched, frequent

Curiosity and anticipation is getting the better of your dog. He really wants you to pay attention to him, take him for a walk or play a game of tag.

Low-pitched, crisp, single

Now, he's telling you that you've gone too far and he wants you to back off and give him a little space. It might be a signal that a training session has gone on too long. If that's the case, take a breather – the dog's attention span has been stretched to its limit and further instruction will fall, for now at least, on deaf ears.

Low, murmuring

An anxious dog will make this sound. He doesn't exactly feel threatened, but he's detected something that he doesn't understand – an unfamiliar sound or scent, for example.

If it's in response to something you've said or done, it means he's frustrated by his inability to understand what you want from him. Change your tactics. If you've been ignoring him, give him a moment of your time.

This is not the sound of defiance, so he won't interpret a change in your behavior as backing down. In fact, a little leeway at this point might avoid a confrontation later.

Single, very urgent, high-pitched yip

The dog may have experienced a moment of pain. Check him over to make sure he hasn't stepped on a sharp object or hurt himself in some other way.

If this develops into a series of yips, especially with a rising pitch, your dog may be in serious pain. If you can't figure out the cause and alleviate it, get him to a vet as quickly as you can.

This is a good example of how sensitive you must be to your own dog's vocal *repertoire* and the situation in which he makes a given sound. This same series of yips, without the sense of urgency, could be an invitation to play.

GROWLS

Quiet, low

The dog means business. He wants you to back off and leave him alone. If this occurs during an encounter with a strange dog, you'd better do as he's telling you.

If it's your dog talking, relax the intensity of what you're doing to let him know that you're listening, but follow up quickly with a short obedience drill to let him know that you're still the boss.

Quiet, low ending with a short, sharp bark

This is an aggressive response to a threat and it's apt to be followed by a snap or a bite. It's a definite red flag, especially if you're dealing with a dog you don't know well. Disarm the situation by remaining calm and still. Slowly move out of the dog's zone of discomfort until he relaxes.

If he's a stranger, leave him alone. If he's yours, don't immediately try to assert your Alpha position by demanding a show of obedience.

Wait until you see definite signs of a mood change before you get in too deep for comfort.

Medium-loud, medium-pitched, growing into a bark

A nervous dog will make this sound, but it isn't a sign of submission. He's prepared to stand up for himself even though he's not sure what the outcome will be.

If the pitch begins to vary, it's a signal that the degree of fear is intensifying – and along with it the likelihood of an aggressive act of self-defense.

Low, murmuring

Unlike other growls, this is a sign of contentment. If you're scratching your dog's ears, he'll make this sound to let you know that he likes what you're doing – and hopes you'll continue.

HOWLS

Long, sustained

This is the wolf sound that Hollywood uses to send chills up the spines of helpless settlers in western movies. In the film, it's usually accompanied by a ferocious lone wolf silhouetted against a full moon.

So much for Hollywood. Far from being a threat, this is the sound a wolf makes when he's become separated from his pack. It's a tormented plea for the rest of his "family" to let him know where they are so he can re-join them.

It's the plaintive, mournful sound your dog makes when he's missing you. Although it's sad and harmless, it can become a major bone of contention among you and your neighbors if it happens every time you leave the house. Later on, when we're dealing with behavior problems and how to solve them, you'll find a few easy tips on how to break your pet of this habit.

Short, with rising pitch

Unlike the preceding howl, this is a happy sound you're likely to hear from your pooch if you've been away for more than a few hours.

Baying

This howl is reserved for hunting dogs when they're onto the scent of their prey. It's a way of letting other dogs in the pack know that the prey is near.

Siren song

This is another canine vocalization that Hollywood has leapt upon – in this case, for comic effect. It's the sound-effect that's used to accompany an annoying singer, usually a shrill soprano.

It's a joining-in form of pack behavior. When one wolf starts to howl, others respond and soon you have a chorus that would drown out the Mormon Tabernacle Choir. Even if your dog isn't much of a singer, he might do this if he hears a police siren wailing in the distance.

WHINES & WHIMPERS

Hesitant whimper

Fear is the message being conveyed. Not the fear of a specific threat, but a vague fear of the unknown, similar to human anxiety. It's the sound dogs typically make in the veterinarian's waiting room. The appropriate response is a soothing pat and soft, encouraging words.

In *The Intelligence of Dogs* (Bantam), psychologist Stanley Coren says that this sound is a carry-over of the mewing sounds puppies make to get their mother's attention when they're cold or hungry.

Persistent whining

This is an extension of the sound described above and it

reflects an intensification of the anxiety. Often, a dog with a seriously full bladder will make this pleading noise while pacing fretfully near the door.

Low-pitched whining

A submissive dog does this to let his rival know he accepts his position in the social pecking order. He's waving a white flag, hoping to avoid a fight in which he expects he'll get pummeled.

It's not a sound that an emotionally healthy and happy dog makes when dealing with his human "pack," although a pooch from the pound who's had to endure abuse in his past might behave this way until you've had a chance to reassure him that his new home will be gentler than the one he's come from.

Note: Any prolonged whining or whimpering may be a sign that your dog is in pain and shouldn't be ignored. Give him the benefit of the doubt and have him checked by a vet before you dismiss this as a sign of a spoiled miscontent.

How To Talk To Your Dog

In the previous section, we mentioned basic obedience training several times. Now It's time to delve a little more deeply into that concept.

It's the most important lesson any dog owner can learn because it will provide you with a basic framework for communicating with your pet that you can extend into all aspects of your relationship with him.

In essence, it establishes the ground rules that will govern how you and your dog will communicate with each other for the rest of your lives together.

Before getting started, recall what we've said about the genetic relationship between dogs and wolves and how that has been modified by thousands of years of domestication in a human environment. You're dealing with an animal whose aggressive instincts, nurtured in the wild, have been muted by countless generations as man's companion and co-worker.

In order to "talk" to him, you have to turn those instincts to your advantage.

By now, you have been armed with a fundamental

55

understanding of canine mentality and the signals – body language and vocalizations – they have at their disposal to let you know what's on their minds.

Now, it's your turn to go to language school, so to speak, to learn how to send signals to your dog in the way most likely to avoid miscommunication and frustration.

We'll proceed step by step through the five basic obedience commands.

By the end of the process, you and your dog will be chatting like the old pals you were meant to be.

And there's a bonus. While you and your dog are tearing down the language barrier that separates you, he'll also be learning to be a well-behaved model canine citizen, a fully integrated member of your family.

Training Preliminaries

To work happily with your dog on the exercises that follow, you'll need some basic equipment. Chances are you already have most of it. If not, it's readily and inexpensively available at all pet stores.

Good equipment is important because without it you'll have difficulty getting a handle on even the simplest techniques. And that will compound the chances of sending the wrong messages to your dog.

The first item on your shopping list should be a six-foot training leash. A retractable leash is NOT acceptable – its flexible length will defeat the purpose of the exercises you and Fido will be working on.

The leash you buy should be made of leather. It's a bit more costly than other materials, but it will last a long time and it's more appropriate for training sessions. A metal leash may hurt your hands and nylon versions aren't flexible enough to do the job.

The width of the leash should be geared to the size of your dog – wider and heavier for larger breeds, lighter and narrower on the smaller ones. In this regard, also make sure to get a leash that fits comfortably in your hand.

What you're looking for is a lead that will give you maximum control with minimum discomfort for both you and your dog.

Next on the list is a training collar and there's a wide variety to choose from. Your best bet is the simple metal type – it's no more than a chain with two rings on the end. Avoid the ones that have extra clasps or hooks. They'll just get in the way and lead to confusion. Make sure the links are small enough so they won't grab your dog's neck, but heavy enough to get his attention.

The purpose of a training collar is not to choke the dog, a dangerous and inhumane gesture. It should tighten and release quickly and easily, exerting enough pressure to keep your dog in check if he's not doing what he's supposed to, but not so much that it will cut off his air supply.

The only effect choking a dog will produce is fear – maybe even panic – and that is precisely the wrong way to build a lasting relationship.

When you buy the collar, bring your dog with you to

ensure a proper fit. (Most large pet superstores allow you to bring your dog inside.) It should go around his neck with enough slack to accommodate your hand easily, no more and no less.

It's crucial that you put the collar on correctly. Thread one loop through the other, slip it over your dog's head and pull it snug. The loop should rest against the back of the dog's neck. If it ends up in front, you run the risk of inadvertently choking him when you tug on it.

In addition, to the 6-foot leash, you'll also need a long line, about 25 to 30 feet in length, to teach your dog to respond to the "Come" command. They're sold in pet stores or you can make your own with a piece of rope and a leash clip.

Training Psychology

Now you can start to put your understanding of Dog Talk to work. It's worthwhile to spend a minute or two reviewing, in point-by-point form, the ground we've covered so far:

1. Your dog is a close relative of an aggressive wild animal who survives by chasing down prey. In other words, your dog is a civilized wolf. He has a built-in urge to control the situation he's in – and you're part of that situation.

2. On the other hand, he's a pack animal who is capable of observing strict rules of social hierarchy.

He will accept you as a surrogate Alpha Dog, but you have to earn that position by getting him to respect your authority rather than fear it.

3. As a pack animal, he knows how to obey instructions, but only if the signals he receives are consistent and given regularly.

4. Similarly, he's constantly sending messages that he expects to be interpreted by you.

Think about it as an old-fashioned vaudeville act. You, as Alpha, are the star. Your dog, as Beta, is the second banana. Like any good team, you have to cooperate with each other or your act will fall flat on its face. There's no room for either of you to play the prima donna.

Your goal is to get your dog to trust you, as Beta Wolves trust the Alpha Wolf to provide them with the means of survival and protection from predators.

The key to achieving this is to be calm, yet authoritative, both in the way you speak and in the way you gesture. There will be moments of intense frustration, hopefully not too many, and when they occur you must never give in to angry outbursts or wimpy wheedling.

Both of these reactions will send a loud and clear trumpet blast to your dog that you're not in control of the situation. And control is what you must never relinquish.

Dogs want to feel that their leader knows what he's doing. They look for a commanding presence who's consistent in both word and deed, and if you can provide that, they'll appreciate you for it.

But they'll pick up instantly on any hint of uncertainty, and if they perceive a vacuum of authority, they'll do one of two things – try to fill it if they're frustrated Alphas or just ignore you if they're contented Betas.

Training Strategy

The two key concepts on which all animal training is based are reward and correction. Reward does NOT mean pampering or permissiveness. Correction does NOT mean punishment.

When your dog does what you want him to, reward him with an encouraging word in a light and friendly tone of voice, accompanied by a brief pat.

Never, never, never reward him with food or you'll end up with a portly pooch who won't give you the time of day unless you have a treat in your hand.

When he doesn't respond as he's supposed to, correct him with a brief, crisp "No" and a firm but meaningful jerk on the leash. Never hit him. It will only breed resentment and can even sabotage any progress you may have made.

Deliver commands in a forceful, even tone of voice. Keep verbal instructions simple, limiting them to single words of one syllable each. Relax your voice a little and allow it to rise slightly in pitch when rewarding a task well done. When issuing the corrective "No," make your voice low and a little louder.

Don't scream, throw things or tug violently on the leash. Don't use baby talk if that's what you do when playing with your dog. This is a training session, not a romp.

Your gestures should be consistent with your voice clear and crisp when you're issuing a command, softer and gentler when you're dishing out praise. Your gestures should also be appropriate to the behavior you're trying to reinforce.

Don't, for example, make a sweeping upward gesture if you want your dog to sit down. Don't make a beckoning motion if you want him to stay put.

At first, perform these hand signals in a somewhat exaggerated way. Just as you are new to Dog Talk and have to look closely for the signs and signals your pet is sending to you, he, too, has to get used to the gestures you'll be using to communicate with him.

Think about learning a new human language. Things go better if the person you're talking to speaks slowly and precisely. Soon, your ear will become attuned and you'll be able to fully comprehend more rapid speech. So, too, will your dog learn to pick up on the most subtle nuances of your body language, but give him a break at the beginning.

If you consistently observe these guidelines, your dog will quickly come to recognize a training session for what it is – work. He'll learn to respond quickly to commands and that's exactly what you want him to do. There'll be plenty of time to play when the session is over.

Dogs, especially young ones, don't have very long attention spans, so keep each individual training session short. Start with 10 or 15 minutes and expand it to half an hour when your dog indicates that he can handle it.

Once he's familiar with the program, he'll be alert

and attentive. Remember what we've learned about Dog Talk: His ears will be forward, his eyes will be focused on you, his mouth will be relaxed.

If his mind begins to wander, he'll gaze absently at his surroundings, become interested in distant movements and sounds, his ears will relax and his body, which should be upright and eager-looking, will get loose.

Pay special attention to his tail. If it's still or moving rhythmically from side to side, he's alert; if it starts to wag eagerly, his mind is on play rather than work.

Finally, pick an area to conduct your training sessions that is as free as possible from distraction. It's a good idea to start indoors, with the radio and television off and with no other people to interrupt the action.

You want all of your dog's attention to be totally focused on you. As Alpha, it's only what YOU do and say that should count. No wolf in the wild would put up with other members of the pack second-guessing his commands and sympathizing if things don't go smoothly.

Ask other family members to leave the room. They'll be able to take part in the training sessions later on and even take on the role of Alpha themselves, but that will come in due time.

If you conduct your training session outdoors, try to work in a fenced-in yard or some other place that offers the necessary seclusion for one-on-one interaction.

Commands

There are just five basic commands to master. Using what you've learned so far about Dog Talk will smooth the way for better communication between you and your dog and significantly reduce the amount of time you'll have to spend practicing.

Work with your dog every day, at the same time of day if you can. The discipline of regular practice will pay off in the long run.

Make a plan of what you intend to accomplish during each session and stick to it. Be realistic, though. You want to end every practice session on a high note of accomplishment and praise and you'll never be able to do that if you bite off more than you can chew.

The positive reinforcement of ending each session in a congratulatory love-fest will make both of you eager for the next one.

But make sure you achieve what you set out to do. Never let your dog off the hook if he becomes restless and inattentive. Like a spoiled child, and a lot of adults, he'll do what he can to shirk his responsibilities and it's your job as Alpha to make him toe the line.

Start every session by getting your dog's attention. In the wild, wolves instinctively pay heed to the Alpha – it's the only way anything gets done. And nothing good will happen between you and your dog unless he's focused on you.

Call his name and clap your hands. Read his Dog Talk for the signs that he's taking you seriously.

COMMAND #1 – SIT

Traditionally, this is the easiest command for a dog to learn because sitting is something he does naturally.

The strange element here is sitting when you want him to, not simply when the mood comes over him. Therefore, you can concentrate on communication rather than the physical movement itself.

1. Having made sure your dog is alert and paying attention to his Alpha (you), take a firm, short hold on the leash with your left hand and bring him to your left side. Switch the leash to your right hand a pull gently upward on the collar while pushing gently downward on his hindquarters with your left.

2. In your firm, even command voice, say "Sit," continuing to exert uniform pressure on his rear end. Don't jerk the leash sharply upward or he'll think you're disciplining him just like his mother used to do by grabbing the back of his neck with her teeth.

3. When your dog sits – and he will – put your hand in front of his face, palm toward him, and say "Stay."

4. Make sure he holds the position for a few seconds and then relax.

5. If he tries to get up before you're ready – and he'll probably do this, too – give one sharp tug on the leash and in your low, sharp correction voice say "No!" If your command sounds like a bark, so much the better. Then repeat until he gets it right.

6. Reward him lavishly with a couple of lively, lilting "Good dogs" and a cheerful pat on the head.

7. Do it again, repeating the praise each time he does it successfully.

COMMAND #2 – STAY

You've already introduced this concept when you told your dog to "Stay" when practicing the previous command. Now it's time to perfect it.

Stay is one of the most important commands your dog will ever learn. It may even save his life in dangerous situations such as, for example, when he feels the urge to act on the perfectly normal canine instinct to chase an animal or person who is running away from him. If he yields to temptation in heavy traffic, the result could be a trip to the emergency veterinary clinic or worse.

Mastering this command is no excuse for allowing your dog to run loose outdoors, but it will give you a safety net should he ever break free from his leash or escape from his fenced-in yard.

1. Execute the "Sit" command and, with the leash in your left hand, make sure your dog is seated by your left side.

2. Calmly and nonchalantly, let the leash fall to the ground and place your left hand, palm open and facing the dog, in front of his face. In your command voice say "Stay."

Now, step around to face him. Do this with as few motions as you can – no excess swinging of your arms and legs and no extra steps or shuffling to get yourself in position. Repeat the command "Stay."

3. Slowly take three steps back and once again repeat the word "Stay."

4. Pause for a second or two. This is plenty at the beginning of your training program. Later on, you'll extend both the time and the distance from the dog.

5. With as few movements as possible, slowly and deliberately return to the starting position so that the dog – hopefully still seated – will be at your left side.

6. Pause a second or two before praising his good performance.

7. If he moves before the end of the exercise, quickly grab the leash and jerk firmly upward on his collar while barking a crisp "No." Then repeat the exercise until he gets it right or until the allotted time for the training session has expired.

8. Only after he has executed this command successfully at least once should you praise him.

This exercise is considerably more difficult for the dog to learn than the "Sit" command. Don't be disappointed or frustrated if it takes a couple of sessions before he gets it right.

Once he learns to do it for a few seconds, gradually increase his sitting-still time to about a minute. Then, increase the distance you step back from him. Ultimately, you should be able to back off a considerable distance while he remains seated for five minutes or longer.

COMMAND #3 – HEEL

Come on, admit it, you've turned green with envy at those dog owners whose pets walk calmly by their sides while yours is lunging at anything that moves and, if he's big and strong enough, dragging you helplessly after him.

The "Heel" command is all it takes for you, too, to walk your dog and maintain your dignity at the same time.

It will take a little more patience than the previous two commands, but the perseverance will pay off in a dog that is a joy, rather than a nuisance, to take on an outing. And being able to go for a relaxed stroll with your pet is one of the great rewards that learning Dog Talk will bring you.

It also cements your position as Alpha. When a dog pulls ahead of you or walks at a pace other than the one you've chosen, he's just doing what nature encourages him to do – taking charge of the situation. But if the two of you are going to be happy together, you're the one who has to call the shots.

The "Heel" command builds on what the dog has learned while getting the hang of sitting and staying, during which he has gotten used to being at your left side in situations where you demand specific types of performance from him.

1. As before, start with the dog seated at your left side. Give him the "Sit" command and persist until he complies.

If things get out of hand, "Sit" is the command

you'll use to get him under control and ready for another try at heeling.

2. Step forward with your left foot. Again, for consistency's sake, always start with the left foot so that your dog will associate this movement with going forward.

3. As you step, in your command voice say "Heel." You may also pat your thigh to add a visual signal to the verbal command. At first, you'll probably also have to give a gentle forward tug on the leash to get your point across, but soon this won't be necessary.

4. Walk at a uniform pace, firmly (but not violently) tugging on the leash every time the dog tries to move at a different speed from the one you've chosen or begins to veer away from your left leg.

5. Proceed only for a short distance, then come to a halt. As you stop, issue the "Sit" command. If your dog complies, praise him. If not, give a mild yank on the leash, chastise him with a firm "No" and keep at it until he does what he's told.

6. Gradually increase the length of your walks until the dog is comfortable with the process and starts and stops smoothly, without cues from the leash.

By this time, you'll be ready to execute a few left and right turns. Do the motion effortlessly and economically, using the leash if you have to bring your dog into the proper "Heel" position after each one.

COMMAND #4 – DOWN

This is the command that will earmark your dog as a perfect canine lady or gentleman. It's the order you'll give when you want him to lie quietly at your feet when you have visitors or the family is involved in an activity that – heaven, forbid – doesn't center around the dog.

1. Once again, start from the "Sit" position, with your dog at your left side.

2. Transfer the leash to your right hand and with your left hand make a broad downward motion in front of your dog's face while turning your body to the left and bending downward from the waist so that you end up eye-level with the dog.

   If your dog is very small you may have to bend your knees as well.

3. While you're doing this, say "Down" in your command voice and move your right hand down far enough so that your dog's collar puts a bit of pressure on the back of his neck.

4. In the beginning, you'll probably have to reinforce these cues by gently pushing down on the dog's shoulders with your left hand.

5. When he assumes a lying position – on his stomach with his paws stretched forward – issue the "Stay" command and release all external pressure, both from the leash and your left hand.

6. Pause for a few seconds and, if he maintains the position, praise him lavishly.

At first, your dog will most likely resist. If so, just increase the downward pressure on his neck and shoulders until he complies. But withhold praise until he holds the position without any physical force.

Once he's able to execute this command easily, you can add the "Stay" command while he's in the down position. As soon as he gives you the signal that he's prepared to remain down, put your hand in front of his eyes and say "Stay" as you move in front of him. Then slowly back away a few feet and repeat the "Stay" command.

After a few seconds, return to his side and praise his good performance.

Finally, when he's "downing" like an old pro, you can teach him to finish this exercise by returning to the comfortable "Sit" position.

Standing by his side, so that he is lying by your left leg, make a broad upward motion with your right hand and say "Sit." A little upward tug on the leash may be required to give him the idea. Once he's sitting quietly by your side, heap on the praise.

COMMAND #5 – COME

When your dog masters this command, you'll have all the proof you need that the two of you have reached a high level of Dog Talk – that you really have found a common language.

"Come" is the command that separates the dogs from the puppies – so to speak – and also firmly establishes the social hierarchy that's so important for your dog's sense of where he fits into the life you share.

Equally important, it will give you peace of mind because you'll know that you can control your dog in just about any situation.

1. Using the "Sit" and "Stay" commands you've already learned, step backward away from your dog to the full-length of his leash, about six feet.

2. Hold still for a second or two to make sure that these commands have "taken."

3. Then, while holding the leash in your extended left hand, make a sweeping gesture toward your chest with your right and say "Come" in your command voice.

4. At the same time, pull gently on the leash to add a little physical reinforcement to the verbal signal.

5. When he obeys, bring him to the "Sit" position and praise him.

It's important when doing this exercise to make sure your voice and gesture are inviting rather than intimidating. Your dog will be reluctant to approach you if you've said or done something that sends the wrong signal that he's going to be punished or chastised.

Graduate to the long lead and when he appears to respond easily to this command, you can finish the exercise by having him come to the "Heel" position.

As your dog progresses from one exercise to the other, begin to combine them all in each training session so that he runs through the whole gamut at least once a day. Sooner than you think, you'll be able to try them without the leash.

So there you have it. Five simple drills and you're well on your way to becoming fluent in Dog Talk. Since you've already learned to read his signals, you've opened a two-way channel of communication between you and your dog that will only improve with time.

And as it improves, the trust and understanding between you will deepen into a lifelong relationship of mutual respect and love.

Your dog will understand what you want when you want it. He'll be eager to follow your lead because you've earned his respect as Alpha.

From your part, you've learned to understand his complicated verbal and physical language so that you can pay him the respect he deserves as a devoted and faithful Beta.

You've acquired the skills and the wisdom to form your own pack and you can slowly integrate other members of your family into it.

The reward for all of you – both human and canine – is years of stress-free happiness.

You and your family will have a devoted and loving companion. Your dog will enjoy the benefit of a pack structure into which he fits perfectly – and that's good for both his mental and physical health.

Now, it's time to take these new communication skills and apply them to two vital areas of dog ownership: picking the right puppy and correcting bad habits.

Putting Dog Talk To Work

Choosing the right puppy is the most important decision a dog owner will ever make. As we've seen, a large part of the dog's temperament has been bred into him before you ever have a chance to work with him to establish the norms of behavior you'll find acceptable.

Picking the Right Puppy

There are three things to consider before you adopt a new pup.

First, you must pick a breed or breed type that suits your own personality and your lifestyle.

For example, if you're looking for a gentle companion dog, a big, rambunctious retriever is not a good choice. If you have kids, a scrappy, nippy terrier might be too aggressive. If you're a neat-freak, a large, slobbery bulldog or mastiff will drive you up the wall.

So be realistic. Don't allow yourself to be unduly influenced by trends or other subjective factors when deciding on the kind of dog to share your home.

Remember, if you're a responsible person – and presumably you are – you're embarking on a long-term relationship when you choose a dog.

The pounds are already too full of tragic animals whose only fault was to be chosen rashly by an owner who didn't pause to think about the implications of his or her hasty decision.

Second, where to get the pup? If you have a specific breed in mind, go to a respected and experienced breeder. The American Kennel Club or a local veterinarian will help you find one.

For reasons we'll deal with shortly, it's better by far to choose a breeder who's close enough to home for you to visit his facilities, check out the parent dogs and meet your prospective puppy before you make a commitment you might come to regret.

Picking your puppy long-distance and having him shipped to you is a sorry second-best alternative.

Rescuing a puppy, or an adult dog, from the pound is a noble thing to do and there are many excellent pets whose lives could – and should – be saved by adoption.

However, you run the risk of getting a dog whose behavior has been warped by a previous neglectful or, worse, abusive owner. These dogs have special problems and need special handling, but this by no means disqualifies the pound as an acceptable place to find your dream pet.

Here again, though, don't be misled by your heart. When you visit the pound to look for a puppy, you'll be greeted by many pairs of sad eyes begging for your at-

tention. In the final section of this book, we'll learn how to use Dog Talk to correct the most common forms of canine misbehavior. These techniques should be adequate to redeem any pound puppy.

Don't lose sight of the type and size of dog you want and be tough-minded when it comes to making a choice. It might be a good idea to leave the kids at home if you think their emotional reactions will overwhelm your better judgment.

Don't buy a puppy from a pet store. They are supplied by appropriately-named "puppy mills," whose owners are in the breeding business only to make a buck. You'll be asking for trouble in the form of an ill-bred, badly raised animal. Medical and behavior problems are likely to surface that will cost you both money and heartbreak.

Patronizing pet shops for anything but supplies fosters this cruel and unscrupulous practice. Vote with your dollars and help to put an end to it. If nobody buys pets from pet shops, the puppy mill operators will soon be out of business.

Sermon over. But no responsible breeder will ever sell a puppy that has medical or behavioral question marks looming over it, so why take a chance when you don't have to.

And this brings us to the third point. Always have a puppy checked by a vet before you make any financial or emotional investment in it. Up-and-up breeders will not object to this.

Most medical problems occurring in puppies are easily

remedied, but there are some that will hamper the dog all its life. It's better to know what you're getting into than have to cope with unpleasant surprises later on.

Meeting Your Puppy

You've decided on a breed, you've been in contact with a local breeder. . . now the day has come to go and take a look at the litter.

Check out the surroundings. Are they clean and professional looking? Are they odor-free? Ask the breeder to give you a tour of the facility. If he balks, you should walk.

Next, chat with him for a while. Ask about his experience as a breeder. How long has he been doing it? How many show titles have his dogs won? What breeds, other than the one you've chosen, has he been involved with?

Trust your instincts. Do you feel comfortable that he "knows dogs?" If not, consider calling a halt to the proceedings until you've had a chance to check, or recheck, his credentials by talking to vets in the area and making a call to the Better Business Bureau.

Ask who he has previously sold pets to and consult with them to see if they are happy. You are about to make an important decision and you can't be too careful.

Now, it's time to meet your puppy's mother and father, if Dad is on the premises. (Often the male parent will have come from another breeder and will have returned home before your visit.)

Put your knowledge of Dog Talk to work. Away from

the presence of her babies, watch how Mom interacts with the breeder.

Since she's a new mom, her protective instincts will make her suspicious of strangers, so don't try to read her behavior from how she reacts to you.

Look carefully at her stance, ear position and tail. Is she confident and friendly?

Be on the lookout for signs of excessive dominance or submission – chances are your puppy will have inherited these traits.

Ask the breeder to put her through a few obedience exercises and observe if she responds willingly and cheerfully to the commands.

Finally, approach her – if she will tolerate this – and pat her to see how she reacts to strangers.

When the breeder takes you to see your puppy-to-be, he'll probably be among his litter mates. This is a good thing because it will give you an opportunity to judge how well-adjusted he is by how he gets along with them.

If you can, watch the litter from a distance at first. They should be feisty, playful and competitive. (Unless they're sleeping, of course.) A puppy who's sitting off by himself or who appears tentative or intimidated is apt to be overly submissive.

When you approach, they all should look alert and curious at the presence of a new creature in their environment. Ears should prick up, Dog Talk for "What's happening here?" A puppy who ignores you or whose ears look droopy or saggy is either frightened or unperceptive.

Reach your hand into their pen and look for the first

one to approach it. This is the sign of a healthy, happy inquisitive animal. He should wag his tail and sniff your fingers. If you're wearing a ring, he may nibble it.

His eyes should be bright and playful, a sign that he regards you as an exciting novelty to be explored.

This is the point that many puppies actually choose their owners instead of the other way around. It could be the beginning of a lasting bond.

But if he won't look into your eyes, it's a sign that he's timid and timid dogs are very hard to deal with.

Did he bark when he scampered over to your hand? A good sign. Did he growl? A sign that he's already striving to be the Alpha Dog in your pack and may be headstrong and difficult to deal with when he gets older.

Pick the puppy up and turn him over on his back. Mother dogs discipline their puppies by flipping them over on their backs, so he might squirm and wriggle a bit. If he does, good. It's a sign that he's got a mind of his own.

But he should calm down and accept your authority after a little tummy scratching. If he doesn't, you may be petting the makings of an aggressive challenger.

Finally, step back and look at his body language in general. The rules you've already learned for interpreting stance in an adult dog also apply to puppies. He should look proud and confident, but not arrogant.

He should also play easily with his litter mates – neither bullying the others or letting the others bully him.

This shows you that he accepts the concept of a social order and has a willingness to fit in, traits that

78

will be vitally important as he grows up. Before bringing a new puppy home, you should prepare for his arrival by buying the things he'll need – and he'll need them as soon as he arrives.

The list is short, simple and not terribly expensive: collar and leash, food and water dish, brush, chew toys and a crate. A child's gate is a good idea if you plan to restrict his access to certain parts of the house. A playpen can accomplish the same end with the added advantage of mobility if you want to move the puppy around the house or take him on a trip with you.

Puppy Training Basics

A commonly asked question is: "How old should a puppy be before he begins training." The customary answer – six months – is wrong.

Your puppy has been in training from the day he was born. And until you brought him home, he had the best trainer in the world – his mother.

So you have an awesome responsibility in taking over from her. But don't fret. Your knowledge of Dog Talk will see you through this challenging time.

Note: A puppy shouldn't be taken from his mother before he's seven weeks old. But you should get him young enough so that you can take advantage of his optimal bonding period that lasts until he is three months.

Housebreaking
The first cloud that darkens the sky for most new dog

owners is the problem of housebreaking. Luckily, his mom has already started this process by discouraging her puppies from messing up their "den." All you have to do is continue the training program that she started.

That's where the crate comes in. It will become your dog's new den, that special place where he'll be spending a lot of quality time with himself and for that reason he won't want to make a mess in it.

Dogs are clean animals (even though anyone who has had to deal with one who's just rolled in a ripe

Is crate training cruel?

Far from it. In fact, one of the kindest things you can do when you bring your new puppy home is to have a crate ready to receive him. When we think of a crate as a prison, we're just being human – too human. To the puppy it represents the security of the den his wolf ancestors grew up in. It reminds him of Mama and his litter mates, in every way a positive experience.

If you use the crate to housebreak your puppy, you'll avoid the recriminations associated with every other method. In effect, he'll housebreak himself because he'll be following a strong instinctive urge not to foul the den where he has to live. His mother has already started to teach him this. All you'll be doing is following in her very wise footsteps.

dead fish will dispute that) and they are appalled at the thought of living in their own filth.

By confining your puppy to a crate when you're away from home or in bed for the night, you've provided him with a reason to housebreak himself. He'll try as hard as he can not to have an "accident" in his crate and if you give him half a chance by letting him outdoors regularly, he won't – maybe right from the very beginning.

In order for this to happen, the crate has to be the right size. It should be big enough for the puppy to turn around with ease, but not so big that he can make a mess in one end and escape from it to the other. That would defeat the purpose entirely.

But, you say, my Great Dane puppy is tiny now, but within six months he'll be big as a giraffe. No problem. Buy a wire crate large enough to accommodate the dog when he's an adult and use readily available partitions to make it the right size for him as he grows.

The wire crate has the advantage of letting your puppy see out when he's confined. For his comfort, you should put a pad on the floor of the crate. You can buy one or make your own from towels.

Now, it's up to you to exercise your command of Dog Talk. Just as a mother wolf will escort her young one from the den when he begins to show the signs of having to relieve himself, so you must watch your puppy for the fidgeting and whimpering that signal he has to go – NOW!

Get him outside quickly, allow him to accomplish his mission, and praise him wildly when he does.

If he can't get out of his cage in time (if you don't get

him out in time) and he messes inside it, don't punish him. He feels bad enough already. Just take him outside, preferably to the spot where he normally goes for this reason, and praise him if he performs.

Then, just as quietly and unemotionally clean out the crate. Be thorough, so no scent of the mistake remains and then go back to business as usual. If you do your job, these mistakes will be few.

A puppy should never be allowed to go more than four hours without a bathroom break. This is a good reason to schedule some vacation time when you bring a new puppy home or make sure someone is available to take him out while you're at work. As he gets older, these necessary outings will become less frequent.

By using the crate to housebreak your puppy, you'll avoid the pitfall of having to deal with messes (yes, plural) when you get home. Even the most friendly owner will convey a subtle sense of annoyance at this and the hyper-sensitive puppy will interpret your negative body language as rejection or punishment.

With the crate, you become the hero, rather than the messenger of doom, as soon as you walk through the door.

Puppy Kindergarten

As for the rest of your puppy's training regimen, easy docs it is the key.

That's not to say that you should pamper him and avoid instruction altogether, but you shouldn't send him to doggy bootcamp either.

The crucial thing is to avoid encouraging bad habits.

It might be amusing when a two-month-old canine tyke nibbles your finger, but it'll be far from a laughing matter if he's still doing it when he's a 90-pound he-dog.

It's better by far to teach your puppy good manners from the start than to have to put him through difficult remedial training later on.

One thing you should definitely do is continue the socialization process that began when he was with his mother and litter mates.

By slow degrees, let him get used to all the members of your family, and trusted strangers as well, so that he won't grow up timid and frightened of humans.

Pick him up a lot. Turn him over on his back – as we mentioned before, this is basic Dog Talk for "I'm the boss" – so that he will accept you as the Alpha and become comfortable with his role as Beta.

Introduce him to as many other dogs as you can. Let them sniff each other and play, but be sure to keep an eye on the situation so your puppy doesn't get bullied.

Practice getting his attention by calling his name and clapping your hands until he looks into your eyes. When training begins in earnest you'll want to be able to keep his mind on business without a struggle.

Get him used to wearing a collar and leash by putting them on him and letting him scamper around the house with the leash trailing behind him.

When both of you are ready for basic obedience training, the leash and collar will then seem like old friends rather than new enemies to him.

Start teaching him table manners by gently pushing

him into a "Sit" position before you turn him loose on his food bowl. Make sure he pauses for a second or two before giving him the OK. It'll prevent him from being an aggressive feeder when he's older.

Use your own judgment about when to start formal obedience training. Most professional trainers won't take dogs less than six months old, but that's to make sure they have had all their shots, not because they're too young to learn.

And, above all, play with him. Puppies, like children, love to play. It's a key part of their lives and your pet lost his natural playmates when he was taken away from his brothers and sisters. Be a willing surrogate and you'll establish a behavior pattern that will keep your dog young at heart for the rest of his life.

Why do puppies chase their tails?

As you might have guessed, they're playing. Dogs are extremely sensitive to motion and when a puppy catches his tail out of the corner of his eye, his natural inclination is to chase it. The behavior is perfectly normal in young dogs, but if it persists in a chronic form into adulthood, it could be the sign of extreme boredom or of a dog with pretty serious emotional problems. Sometimes, a canine counselor is called for to determine the cause – and the cure.

Problems &
How To
Fix Them

"There's no such thing as a bad dog." How many times have you – as you stand there with your tattered sweater in one hand, a chewed up shoe in the other, a sofa ripped to shreds – heard that one? It's not the first thing a dog owner who's just arrived home to find her house in chaos wants to hear.

But it is, nevertheless, true. No dog is evil; no dog misbehaves just to irritate you, and no dog – no matter how much of a canine juvenile delinquent he may appear to be – is bad.

Dogs are complex creatures, part instinctive and part socialized. These two aspects of their personalities live in a somewhat uneasy truce. Sometimes instinct gets the upper hand and the dog behaves in a way that appears to be "bad."

But he's just doing what comes naturally. Unfortunately, he may be doing it at the worst possible time and in the worst possible place.

For example, when Joan's poodle chews her favorite

cashmere sweater into a comfy bed and curls up and goes to sleep on it while Joan is at work, the pooch isn't making a fashion statement. All she's trying to do is get as close as she can to something that reminds her of her human "mother."

Since a family photograph has no meaning for a dog, he's drawn to something he can relate to with his sense of smell. Hence, a frequently worn article of clothing.

To punish him for this will only confuse him because he doesn't realize he's done anything wrong.

And that's exactly where serious behavioral problems begin: When an owner misinterprets what his dog does and reacts in a way that leads to confusion and resentment – and ultimately a loss of trust on the part of the dog.

Similarly, when Harry banishes his rottweiler to the backyard for barking, the dog, who likes to be outdoors, thinks he's being rewarded and will bark all the more.

But with an understanding of Dog Talk, this sort of miscommunication need never occur.

With that in mind, let's look at a few of the most common canine "felonies and misdemeanors" and see how Dog Talk can lead us to the solutions.

My dog urinates when I come into the house.

This is submissive urination, a sign of subordination. An Omega Wolf will urinate when he sees the Alpha Wolf approaching to let the dominant animal know that there's no need for an aggressive display of his superior social status.

Remember your Dog Talk vocabulary and observe your pet for other signs of submissive behavior. Does he put his tail between his legs when you draw near? Does he refuse to make eye contact with you?

If the urination falls into a submissive pattern, check your body and verbal language to make sure you're not inadvertently projecting a threatening image.

Enter the house slowly and quietly – a boisterous, overly enthusiastic greeting will just trigger the behavior you're trying to correct.

Get down to your dog's eye level and let him approach you. Allow him to sniff your face, maybe even lick it. Gradually, he'll stop thinking of you as a threat and the problem will disappear.

Don't mistake this type of urination for another all-too-common problem – marking urination. Dogs have a strong instinct to mark their territory with urine to let other dogs know of their presence. It's a major method of dog-to-dog communication.

Dogs have a tendency to do this whenever they encounter new surroundings, especially if you're visiting another dog's home. Or when you bring new elements into already-familiar surroundings, such as when you bring a new piece of furniture into the house.

The way to correct it is to reactivate the crate you used to housebreak your dog when he was a puppy. A little refresher course is in order. Pre-crate the dog if a new sofa is on the way and bring the crate with you when you take the dog on a trip.

Do dogs feel guilt?

You come home from work and you just know by
the way your dog looks at you that he's done
something wrong. You haven't said or done anything to indicate that you're about to chastise him
and, yet, his body language tells you he's hiding a
shameful secret. Sure enough, a quick inspection
reveals your favorite sweater chewed to shreds.
Was the "hang-dog" a tacit admission of guilt?
Yes, in a way. If the dog has been scolded for
similar behavior in the past, his memory is good
enough to tell him that he's in for another dressing
down as soon as evidence of his most recent
crime comes to light.

My dog likes to jump up on people.

When a dog jumps up, he's trying to greet you at eye
level. It's a nuisance in small dogs and a danger in
large ones. Since he's just trying to be friendly, punishment is not only inappropriate, it's guaranteed to lead
to confusion and even hostility.

Most problems occur when you come home after an
absencc of a few hours or more. Try to disarm the situation by keeping your arrival low-key until the dog's
level of excitement subsides.

If this doesn't work, take the dog's paws in your
hands and slowly but firmly place them on the floor while

saying either "No" or "Off." Don't say "Down" – as you recall from the section on basic obedience training that command has a specific meaning and you don't want your dog to associate it with a reprimand.

Without losing your temper, repeat this procedure until the dog quiets down. When he does, praise him lavishly. You may have to re-enact this drill for several days before the dog "gets it."

When the dog stops jumping up on you, have each family member do the corrective procedure until the dog is well-behaved with all of you. By that time, the problem should be solved. However, if there are one or two people who visit you frequently, you may have to "train" them as well.

My dog begs at the table until I give him some food from my plate.

You are the culprit here. Even though you disapprove of his begging, you reward him with food every time he does it. Talk about mixed signals!

The Dog Talk message is this: Your dog thinks of your family as his pack and he wants to be part of the action. Food is a basic instinct, so he heads for the table every time the family assembles so he can share in the "pack meal."

He first reared up on his hind legs just to get a better view. When you started giving him food, he took it as a reward and it re-enforced the behavior.

Here's what to do. Issue the "Down" command and keep your dog lying politely by your feet until dinner is over. Then give him his own dinner in his usual place – well away from the dining table.

There's another good Dog Talk reason for feeding the dog after you and your family eat. In a pack, who gets to eat first? The Alpha Wolf, that's who. If you feed your dog before yourself, it will re-enforce his tendencies toward dominant behavior.

My dog barks and howls so much the neighbors are going to lynch him – or me!

Barking is a normal canine activity, like eating and smelling, so you'll never get him to stop entirely. The result would be a very neurotic dog.

But excessive barking is usually due to loneliness and boredom. An under-employed dog will take it up as a way to pass the time until something more interesting happens.

The Dog Talk way to get this annoying habit under control is to spend quality time with your dog. Take him for long walks. Play with him a lot. If the dog is happy and tired when you leave him alone, he'll sleep rather than bark.

Dogs are social animals. If they're confined in a house or yard by themselves, they'll bark to attract canine companionship. Take him regularly to a park, where he can satisfy this need by meeting other dogs in a controlled and safe environment.

Excessive barking is a difficult problem to correct, but this Dog Talk technique should work if you have the patience to re-enforce the lesson over a few weeks.

Allow the dog to bark once or twice, say when the post-man is approaching. This is a natural warning function and shouldn't be restricted.

Praise him and then immediately correct him by saying "Quiet" in a very loud and commanding voice.

When he stops, praise him. He gradually learns to associate more than one or two barks with chastisement and silence with reward.

Once you begin this program, make sure you don't unconsciously affirm the unwanted behavior by giving in to the dog immediately if he barks for food or to be let out.

Meanwhile, beg the neighbors to be indulgent. You won't be able to correct this problem overnight.

Can dogs and cats ever get along together?

Sure, but you're dealing with the canine's powerful chase instinct and to get it under control requires a lot of practice, especially if the dog is a member of a breed, like the terrier, that has been molded to chase and kill smaller animals.

Whatever the breed, don't just bring a cat into your home and expect things to work out fine. The chase instinct is so strong very few dogs will be able to resist the temptation.

The following exercise will help, but you'll need to enlist the help of a family member or friend.

Put the dog on his leash and bring him to the "Sit" position by your side. Have your assistant bring the cat into the room, holding her in a traveling cat cage. If the dog makes a move toward the cat, correct him immediately and make him "Sit" once more.

When he remains comfortably by your side, ask the assistant to take a step closer. Repeat this until dog and cat are nose to nose and the dog shows no signs of wanting to pounce.

Now, walk the dog around the room on the leash and correct him every time he lunges at the cat. Keep this up until you're comfortable he's getting the message.

Drop the leash, but keep it within reach, grabbing it and correcting any motion toward the cat.

They may never be best of friends, but in time they should be able to live in relative peace. However, until you're absolutely sure, never leave them together unattended. Crate them in turn, if you have to, until your dog has proven he's been thoroughly "cat-proofed."

What about dogs and small children?

The same technique you used to train your dog to accept a cat will help him get used to a child. But the child also must be taught to respect the dog as a legitimate member of your family and not a toy.

Supervise interactions between your dog and all children until you're convinced the child knows some basic Dog Talk or at least can be trusted to follow these rules:

- Never hit, kick or ride the dog. Never pull his ears or tail or tease him in any other way.

- Stay away from the dog while he's eating. Protecting his food is a basic instinct of every dog.

🦴 Don't stare directly into the dog's eyes. He may interpret it as a challenge and react aggressively.

🦴 Don't run toward or away from the dog or make any sudden, threatening movements around him. These actions might trigger his chase instinct or self-protection behavior.

Note: As a general rule of thumb: Don't leave dogs alone with young children. The consequences could be disastrous.

My dog keeps getting into the garbage and tossing it all over the house.

Dogs are curious creatures and they'll explore whenever they have the opportunity.

Since they're also clever, it's unlikely that your pet will attack the garbage can while you're around, and punishing him after the fact won't do anything to help because he's not going to associate the punishment with the crime.

There are sprays available that are supposed to make the garbage unpalatable, but if the dog doesn't mind the taste of garbage to begin with – they have far fewer taste buds than humans do – he's hardly likely to be bothered by a spray, no matter how off-putting it smells to us.

The only thing you can do to stifle this upsetting behavior is to put the garbage can well out of your dog's reach. Make sure he keeps up with his obedience exercises – they'll help to make him a better adjusted citizen in general.

My dog just won't accept me as the boss.

You have a super-dominant pet on your hands who will challenge your authority every time you let him. The key phrase is "let him." Never allow a single instance of dominant behavior pass uncorrected.

The obedience exercises you've already learned are the crux of the solution to this problem. Remember, the logic behind obedience training is that you're the Alpha Dog and your pet is the Beta Dog.

Every time he challenges you, put him through the exercises one by one. While calming him down, it will remind him of his position in the pack.

Be consistent. Never let him get away with unacceptable behavior. Obedience train him every time – it only takes a minute or two.

My dog likes to chew shoes and clothing.
It's getting expensive.

Your dog likes to chew everything. This mimics eating – his favorite thing – and the munching motion feels good in itself.

You're not going to win this one if by winning you mean getting your dog to stop chewing entirely. You must provide him with a supply of chew toys and, since he can't tell the difference between what he's supposed to chew and what he isn't, you'll have to keep your shoes and clothes out of reach.

My dog likes to sleep on my bed.

Sure he does. Your scent is all over it and reminds him of his maternal den, which he associates with se-

curity and happiness. Go with the flow and put a piece of your old clothing in the place where you want him to sleep (his crate or doggie bed, for example) and praise him when he lies down on it. Don't wash it, however. Your scent is what makes it attractive.

My dog is good when I'm at home, but goes on a destructive rampage when he's alone.

Ah, separation anxiety – a real toughie to deal with, but not impossible if you know Dog Talk.

Solitude is not a normal state for your very social dog. When you're away, he misses you, pure and simple. And chances are, you foster this behavior by being especially cuddly and affectionate when you're at home.

Instead, substitute obedience training for the hugs and kisses. Your dog will get the interaction he wants, but not the coddling he misses when you're gone. To you, it may seem cold, but to him it provides the structure he needs to maintain his emotional equilibrium.

Also, tone down your excitement when you arrive and depart. If you maintain a calm atmosphere when you come and go, you'll be less likely to instigate an emotional reaction when you're gone.

My dog snaps at me when I go near his food dish.

Food aggression is a common behavior problem, rooted in the basic instinct that tells your dog that if he doesn't eat he'll die. Therefore, he will protect his food at all costs.

The answer is to associate feeding with some other

activity that makes it clear to him that you're the boss and it's you – not he – who will decide when he eats.

Before feeding your dog, put him through his obedience paces. When the drill is over, make him sit until you put his food dish in front of him. Correct him if he jumps at it.

When the bowl is safely down, release him from the "Sit" command with a friendly "Good boy" and let him eat. When he's finished, even if there's food left, make him sit until you remove the bowl. Then, praise him for his good behavior.

This way, he'll remember that you're the Alpha and, as such, you get to determine who eats when. Your control will make sense to him and he'll willingly follow your lead.

We got a new dog from the pound and our old dog won't accept him. They get into fights all the time.

You're probably forgetting a basic element of Dog Talk and pack behavior – one of your two dogs is going to be dominant. Watch them for signs of aggressive and submissive behavior and determine which of them has assumed the position of Alpha.

They'll work this out between themselves – without any help from you – and they'll probably do it without fighting. The trouble starts when you don't observe the pecking order and try to treat both dogs as equals.

The dominant one resents this and will fight to assert his authority over the other dog.

Remember, a pack is not a democracy – the dogs are not equals in their eyes and they shouldn't be in yours.

Once you've determined which dog is dominant, greet him first when you walk through the door. Allow him to eat first, horde toys and precede the more submissive dog through doors. Peace and order will quickly be restored and both dogs will be happy that their social arrangement is being respected.

My dog cowers and cringes all the time.

You have a super-submissive pooch on your hands. This problem crops up often in pound dogs who may have suffered abuse at the hands of their previous owners.

Such a dog will flinch every time you raise your voice or advance toward him. The problem is one of the most difficult to solve, but with Dog Talk, it's not impossible to turn this sad creature into a dog who can enjoy his life and be a good companion to you.

You have to show the dog that the world doesn't have to be a threatening place. And there are two steps to achieving this goal.

First, work on basic obedience training to help him learn to trust you as a compassionate Alpha. Be especially cautious when you correct his mistakes and praise him lavishly – really go overboard – when he does well.

Once, he's learned to trust you, have a family member or friend take over the obedience training chore so that the dog can learn that you're not the only human on Earth who'll treat him decently.

Now, you're ready to move on to step two.

Take the dog on as many outings to as many different places as you can.

Expose him to as much variety as he can handle. It may be slow going at first, but if you have the patience, he'll soon begin to loosen up.

Watch for Dog Talk signs of confidence – alertly looking around, eagerness to meet other dogs, a more comfortable gait when he walks. All these things will tell you that he's making progress.

Be sure to prevent other people and dogs from behaving too aggressively at first. Avoid crowds, for example, until the dog begins to exhibit less Omega behavior on a regular basis.

Resist the urge to pat and comfort him when he has moments of insecurity. He'll only interpret this as praise and try to give you what he thinks you're looking for by relapsing.

Do you have a furry friend who makes your life worth living? We'd love to hear all about him or her. Send your story to:

DOG TALK
AMI Mini Mags
5401 N.W. Broken Sound Blvd.
Boca Raton, FL 33487-3589